Did

REA

A MISCELLANY

Compiled by Julia Skinner

With particular reference to the work of Martin Andrew

THE FRANCIS FRITH COLLECTION

www.francisfrith.com

First published in the United Kingdom in 2005 by The Francis Frith Collection®

This edition published exclusively for Oakridge in 2010 ISBN 978-1-84589-523-5

British Library Cataloguing in Publication Data

Did You Know? Reading - A Miscellany
Compiled by Julia Skinner
With particular reference to the work of Martin Andrew

The Francis Frith Collection
Frith's Barn, Teffont,
Salisbury, Wiltshire SP3 5QP
Tel: +44 (0) 1722 716 376
Email: info@francisfrith.co.uk
www.francisfrith.com

Printed and bound in Malaysia

Front Cover: **READING, THE ARCADE c1900** R13302p

The colour-tinting is for illustrative purposes only, and is not intended to be historically accurate

CONTENTS

INTRODUCTION

The busy modern town of Reading stands on historic foundations. The Romans had farms and villas in the area, and Reading Museum in Blagrave Street has many fascinating finds from local archaeological excavations. The Danes used Reading as a winter fortress during their raids on England, apparently over a long period, as the Anglo-Saxon Chronicle mentions them over-wintering there in 871 and 1006. In the Middle Ages the town was an important commercial centre for the cloth trade. Reading had a Cluniac abbey founded by Henry I in 1121, which became his favourite monastic establishment and was also his place of burial.

Reading had an ancient castle, probably an earthwork, although its site is not definitely known. In the early Middle Ages King Stephen constructed another, short-lived, castle at Reading during the period of conflict between himself and his cousin Matilda, which was destroyed in around 1152 or 1153. Reading was also the scene of several bitter conflicts during the Civil War.

Reading's early settlement was established on the banks of the River Kennet away from the Thames water-meadows, but the town expanded rapidly in the 19th century with the coming of the railway, and developed into an industrial centre. Blake's Lock Museum, on the banks of the River Kennet, has interesting and colourful displays of life and work in 19th- and 20th-century Reading.

READING, THE CAVERSHAM HOTEL 1910 62208

In recent years Reading has attracted a growing population, centred around new employment areas such as the computer and insurance industries. Reading University, on the south-western edge of the town, is known for its agriculture and meteorology courses, and is also home to the Museum of Rural Life. For younger residents all over the country the annual Reading pop festival is a highlight in the year.

Despite its modern development, Reading is still rich in many interesting buildings and is well worth exploring. The town's story is full of interesting characters and events, of which this book can only provide a glimpse.

BERKSHIRE DIALECT WORDS AND PHRASES

'Reddin' - correct pronunciation of Reading!

'Cheeselog' - a woodlouse.

'Deedy' - careful.

'Dout' - to put out a fire.

'Footer' - to cry.

'Shucketty' - shaky.

'Pikked' - pointed.

'Bottom' - a valley.

'Tarblish' - tolerable.

'Snook' - stolen.

'Wuut' - a mole.

'Vorights' - opposite.

HAUNTED READING

Waltington House in Reading is believed to be haunted by the ghost of Captain Edward Purvis, who fought in the Peninsula War. During his lifetime he would sit at his window smoking a pipe, wearing a red military jacket, and his ghost has been seen doing the same on several occasions.

The Roebuck Hotel on the A329 is haunted by the ghost of an old Admiral who is believed to have died in the building in the 18th century. His ghost rearranges furniture, locks doors and windows and knocks on the walls. His footsteps have also been heard pacing the corridors late at night.

Sightings of a ghostly blue car have been reported on Berkeley Avenue. Driven by a red-haired lady with an elegant hairstyle, the car has no lights and makes no sound.

The Sun Inn in Castle Street is reputedly haunted by three ghosts, that of a monk downstairs and those of a lady and a young girl upstairs.

READING MISCELLANY

Originally the outer gate of Reading Abbey was attached to the south flank of St Lawrence's Church. The church was enlarged in 1196; this was probably connected with the establishment of the Hospitium of St John the Baptist. The Perpendicular tower has polygonal buttresses and a tall arch to the nave, and a lower one to the north aisle embraces the tower. The arcade itself was rebuilt in 1522. The interior has additions throughout, although some have now gone: an arcade of six arches known as Blagrave's Piazza along the west half of the south wall was demolished in 1868.

Designed by Henry Woodyer in High Victorian Gothic style, Christ Church (see page 7) was built in 1861-62 and enlarged in 1874. It is large and imposing, with a tower and spire 165 feet high. Inside, the church is a tour-de-force of Victorian inventive re-interpretation of the medieval Decorated style, with exuberant arcade capitals with friezes of richly foliaged arches, and reticulated tracery infill to the upper part of the chancel arch. Henry Woodyer obviously enjoyed himself when designing this wonderful church.

Until about 1600 the wide street of St Mary's Butts was used for archery practice. St Mary's Church contains some interesting monuments. That of William Kendrick (1635) has two kneeling figures facing each other. John Monk (1809) is commemorated with an expiring man in a chair, fortified by a standing figure of Faith.

READING, GREYFRIARS' CHURCH 1904 52009

The Greyfriars (the Franciscan order) arrived in 1234 to a frosty reception from the Abbot of Reading Abbey, who grudgingly gave them marshy land by the River Thames on which to settle. The area proved too unhealthy, and in 1285 the Archbishop of Canterbury intervened; the friars were given a new site at the end of what is now Friar Street, and their new church was built by 1311. The church was ruinous and roofless by 1850, and was virtually rebuilt in 1863.

In 1006 the Anglo-Saxon Chronicle describes with grim humour a Danish army moving from the Isle of Wight to 'their well stocked food depot at Reading, and as usual kindled their beacons' - in other words, they burned every town and village they passed through.

Not far from Reading is Pangbourne. The 17th-century Swan Inn, on the outskirts, is where Kenneth Grahame reputedly wrote most of his classic children's story 'The Wind in the Willows'. At one time the county boundary between Oxfordshire and Berkshire ran right through the middle of this building, dividing the two bars. The licensing laws differed either side of the line, and closing time would vary by as much as half an hour. Keen drinkers simply moved from one county to the other by taking their drink into the other bar.

One of Reading's more familiar landmarks is Caversham Bridge, which connects the town centre with Caversham and Henley. This bridge was opened in 1926, replacing the iron bridge of 1869 (shown on page 26-27). An earlier bridge played a key role in the Civil War, and King Charles I and his nephew Prince Rupert engaged in a fierce fight here against the Earl of Essex in 1643.

READING, CAVERSHAM BRIDGE c1955 R13048

READING, THE MAIWAND MEMORIAL 1890 27139

This extraordinary monument (above) in Forbury Gardens is dominated by a colossal cast iron lion weighing 16 tons, erected in 1884 to commemorate eleven officers and 318 other ranks of the 66th (Berkshire) Regiment who died in the Second Afghan War of 1879-80, particularly for their rearguard action at Maiwand. In this photograph the memorial is decked with wreaths and garlands for the anniversary, close enough in time to the events for some of the people in the view to be relatives of those named, or actual veterans of that terrible campaign.

The Great Western Railway arrived at Reading in 1840.

The first documentary reference to Reading is found in the Anglo-Saxon Chronicle for AD 871: 'In this year rode the host (the Danish army) to Reading in Wessex … then ealdorman Aethelwulf opposed them at Englefield and fought against them and won the victory. Four days afterwards King Aethelred and Alfred [later The Great] his brother led great levies there to Reading, and fought against the host; and great slaughter was made there on either side, and ealdorman Aethelwulf was slain, and the Danes had possession of the field of slaughter'. The Danish army over-wintered in Reading in AD 871, and in the spring of AD 872, having thoroughly pillaged the whole area, moved on to London.

READING, BROAD STREET 1913 65910

In early times Reading was a significant settlement of strategic importance, dominating as it did the valley of the Rivers Thames and Kennet. It was certainly an Anglo-Saxon borough or 'burh', and the Domesday Book entry for Reading tells us that it had a market and its own mint for coinage; pennies from the reign of Edward the Confessor are known.

Reading Abbey was founded in 1121 by Henry I, the fourth son of William the Conqueror. He was nicknamed 'Beauclerc' (fine clerk) because, unlike most nobles of the time, he could actually sign his own name. Although he is believed to have fathered around 23 illegitimate children, his only legitimate male heir was drowned in the 'White Ship' tragedy. The grieving king invited the Cluniac order of monks to Reading and showered the new monastery with land and gifts, although at some time in the 13th century it became a Benedictine abbey.

Until the monasteries were dissolved by Henry VIII in the late 1530s, Reading Abbey was one of the most powerful and rich in England. The last Abbot, Hugh Faringdon, a former friend of King Henry, was hanged, drawn and quartered for high treason in November 1539 because he would not acknowledge King Henry's supremacy over the Pope.

READING, THE ABBEY, THE CHAPTER HOUSE 1904 52018

Very little remains of Reading's abbey, as much of it was taken down for re-use as building materials elsewhere in the town, including the rebuilding of St Mary's Church in St Mary's Butts in the 1550s. What does survive is impressive: the towering flint core of the south transept walls and east chapel, the doorway into the cloister from the nave, the chapter house, and some of the buildings along the east wall of the cloister east walk. These have all been robbed of almost every piece of dressed stone cladding, so that what can still be seen is the flint core of the walls, which were massively thick.

There are a number of timber-framed Tudor and 17th-century houses in Reading, such as 27-28 Market Place.

The growth of Reading and its prosperity in the Middle Ages owed much to its wealthy abbey. The town developed a strong wool and cloth trade which declined from the 17th century on, although sail making and a silk industry maintained the link with textiles for many years.

One of Reading's major employers was Sutton Seeds, founded in 1806, which moved away from the town to Torquay in 1974.

READING, SUTTON SEEDS 1912 64639

Reading, with its strategic importance as a crossing place on the River Thames, had an eventful Civil War, changing hands several times. It was the first town in England to be besieged in the war, in April 1643 by Parliamentary forces, and extensive earthworks surrounded the town. The Royalists inside the town eventually

surrendered, but much damage was done to Reading during the siege, including the tower of St Giles' Parish Church, which had been used as a Royalist gun position (at that time the church did not have a steeple - this was added c1873). Of the defences only the tree-clad mound in Forbury Gardens remains.

READING, THE ARCADE c1900 R13302

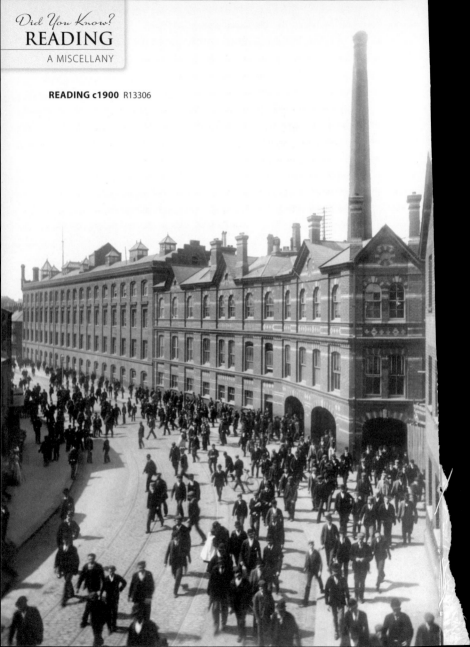

READING c1900 R13306

During the 17th and 18th centuries breweries, maltings, fulling mills and brick and tile making replaced the woollen cloth industry, and the town prospered and expanded. Mills, warehouses and industry developed along the Kennet; the river was canalised from the 1720s, despite riots and violent opposition, and later, by an Act of Parliament in 1794, the Kennet and Avon Canal was begun. Completed in 1810, it led to new prosperity and expansion for the town.

The expansion of Reading in the 19th century caused many of the old Georgian buildings to be demolished and replaced, which is why Reading has so much Victorian architecture, such as the former McIlroys store (1903) in Oxford Road, and Queen Victoria Street. In the last two decades of the 19th century many shops and buildings were rebuilt in a Dutch gabled style, with soaring complex gables with pinnacles and ball or other finials.

Despite the worst efforts of the 1960s town planners and the demands of modern traffic, Reading still has many interesting and historic buildings: it retains the pre-18th-century street plan, and has about 800 listed or protected buildings.

One of Reading's interesting buildings is its railway station, built in 1840 in Italianate style.

The statue of King Edward VII (see page 15) was presented to the town in 1902 to mark the king's coronation. It now stands in a busy traffic island, surrounded by flowerbeds.

The area now known as Forbury Gardens survived as open space because the citizens had rights to hold fairs and events in the former monastery forecourt. However by the 19th century it had become a rubbish tip and dung heap; it was bought by the Council in the 1850s to be laid out as a public park much as it is today.

Caversham Heights lies to the north of the Thames, and began to expand up the valley slopes when Caversham became a fashionable suburb of Reading.

The pond at the foot of the hill in Prospect Park is heart-shaped in plan, and was laid out by Benjamin Child, the then owner of Prospect Hill House (now known as the Mansion House) in memory of his wife Frances; it is claimed that she challenged him either to marry her or fight her in a duel, and he took the safest option!

Reading boasts one of England's finest folk museums - the Museum of English Rural Life. Its collection covers all aspects of traditional country life, from bee-keeping to weaving.

READING, FRIAR STREET, THE TOWN HALL AND ST LAWRENCE'S CHURCH 1923 74440

Reading's fine Victorian Gothic Town Hall was designed by Alfred Waterhouse and built in 1875. Waterhouse was the architect of London's Natural History Museum, and was a Reading resident. The curious onion-domed extension to the Town Hall seen in the photograph above, not part of Waterhouse's original design, has since been demolished.

Until 1911 Caversham had always been in Oxfordshire. The merging of the village into the borough of Reading was strongly resisted by the residents of Caversham.

Reading Museum contains the finds from the archaeological excavations at nearby Silchester. This was the Roman administrative capital for the local area, and its Roman name was Calleva Atrebatum, named for the dominant Celtic tribe in the region, the Atrebates.

At the centre of Reading's Market Place is the Simeon Monument, designed by the great architect Sir John Soane, and erected in 1804. It was given to the town by Edward Simeon, a former Governor of the Bank of England, 'erected and lighted forever at the expense of Edward Simeon as a mark of affection to his native town'.

READING, MARKET PLACE 1870 R13001

This view from the south bank towpath shows the 1869 iron bridge. This replaced an earlier bridge which, curiously, was timber and iron northwards towards the then Berkshire boundary in midstream, and stone for the then Oxfordshire north half, the result

of a cross-border dispute. Part of the 'deal' whereby Oxfordshire surrendered Caversham to Reading in 1911 was the rebuilding of the 1869 bridge, which was found to be sub-standard. The new bridge was opened in 1926 by the Prince of Wales.

CAVERSHAM BRIDGE 1904 52027

READING, THE ABBEY RUINS, A FIREPLACE 1910 62207

The fireplace seen in the photograph on page 28, possibly from the Abbot's lodgings, was placed in the Norman south transept but has since been removed to safer quarters.

Reading was the site of the only significant fighting during the Glorious Revolution of 1688, which put William of Orange and his wife Mary (daughter of James II) on the throne. The Catholic James II sent an army to Reading to cut off the march of William and his Protestant forces. The people of Reading sent a message to William asking for help, and 250 of his troops attacked the forces of King James, which retreated.

The name 'Reading' probably comes from the Anglo-Saxon for 'The Place of Readda's People'. In the eighth century the town was known as Readingum. Another possibility is that the name may be Celtic, 'Rhydd-Inge' or 'The Ford over the River'.

In the 19th century the town was famous for 'Reading Sauce'. This was described as a sharp sauce flavoured with onion, spices and herbs, much like Worcestershire sauce. In Jules Verne's 'Around the World in Eighty Days' Phileas Fogg enjoys 'a side dish, a boiled fish with Reading sauce of first quality'.

John Betjeman said of Reading in the 1930s: 'Few towns are less prepossessing at first glance than Reading…but few towns better repay exploration'.

On the wall of the Chapter House of Reading Abbey is a plaque commemorating the fact that one of the earliest recorded pieces of music was written down at the abbey: 'Sumer is icumen in' (Summer is a-coming in). A four-part harmony 'round' dating from 1225, the original manuscript is now kept in the British Library.

> *Sumer is icumen in*
> *Lhude sing cuccu.*
> *Groweth sed and bloweth med*
> *And springth the wude nu.*
> *Sing cuccu!*
> *Awe bleteth after lomb*
> *Lhouth after calve cu:*
> *Bulluc sterteth*
> *bucke verteth,*
> *Murie sing cuccu!*

The only complete survival from Reading's abbey is this splendid gateway (see page 31) which led from the great forecourt, now partly Forbury Gardens, into the monastic precincts. In serious decay by the 19th century, it partly collapsed in 1861 but was reconstructed by George Gilbert Scott in 1869. Nowadays it leads into office precincts rather than monastic ones.

READING, OXFORD STREET 1913 65912

The huge building on the right of the photograph above, the former McIlroys, opened in 1903 and was known locally as Reading's Crystal Palace for its huge shop windows. The top storey has now been rebuilt in simpler style. At this time Oxford Street was known as Oxford Road.

In medieval times Reading Abbey held over 230 sacred relics, including the hand of St James.

Basildon Park, at Lower Basildon near Reading, was used as a location for the 2005 film 'Pride and Prejudice', starring Keira Knightly.

In Thomas Hardy's novels, Reading is disguised as 'Aldbrickham'. In 'Jude the Obscure' Jude and Sue lived in Aldbrickham, where they had a monumental masonry business.

In June 1909 this memorial cross (below) was erected to commemorate King Henry I, the founder of Reading Abbey, who was buried before the high altar in 1136. Beyond is St James's Roman Catholic Church of 1840, built in the Norman style by Pugin, later a passionate advocate of Gothic architecture.

READING, FORBURY GARDENS 1910 62206

33

The famous mathematician John Blagrave was probably born near
Reading in 1561, the son of John and Anne Blagrave of Bulmershe
Court near Sonning. He was educated at Reading School, and
published four influential books on mathematics. He died in 1611

READING, FORBURY GARDENS AND ST JAMES'S CHURCH 1896 37168

and is buried in St Lawrence's Church. His lands at Southcote Manor, now in the Reading suburb of Southcote, passed to his nephew Daniel Blagrave, who was one of the signatories of the death warrant of King Charles I.

READING, BROAD STREET 1893 31721

Broad Street was formerly the sheep market, when Reading was a prosperous wool town; it later became the commercial and shopping focus of the Victorian town. The arched and pedimented building halfway along on the left of the photograph above was the old covered market entrance.

The 17th-century side-saddle traveller Celia Fiennes commented: 'Reading is the shire town, its pretty Large and accomodated for travellers being a great Road to Gloucester and ye West Country, but it is very dear'.

Lawrence of Arabia, real name T E Lawrence, lost the first draft of his account of the war in the desert, 'Seven Pillars of Wisdom', at Reading station.

The Waterstone's bookshop in Broad Street is sited in a skilfully converted ex-nonconformist chapel dating from 1707.

During the Second World War only one German bomb hit the town, which severely damaged the Market Arcade, a terra cotta and brick Jacobean-style extravagance.

READING, THE ARCADE 1896 37158

READING, ON THE THAMES 1913 65921

SPORTING READING

Reading Football Club were formerly nicknamed 'the Biscuitmen', but are now known as 'the Royals'. Since 1998 they have been based in the new 24,084-capacity Madejski stadium, which is named after the chairman, John Madejski.

In March of each year up to 12,000 runners take part in the Reading Half Marathon, which is run through the streets of the town.

Reading has three senior semi-professional ruby clubs: Reading RFC, Redingensians RFC and Reading Abbey RFC. The Zurich Premiership team London Irish also play their home matches at Reading's Madejski stadium.

Thomas (Tommy) Martin was one of Reading's most interesting sportsmen. Born in Reading in 1916, he was one of the most successful pre-war black boxers in Britain. He turned professional in 1933 and had great success. In 1939 he won every fight, including a points win over future British Heavyweight Champion Jack London. Martin was unable to fight for the British title, though, because of a colour bar. The bar was lifted in 1947, but Martin had retired five years earlier.

Reading's speedway team, the Racers, had a dramatic rise from nowhere in their early days. The club was founded in 1968, and six years later they were Division One Champions, the best team in the country.

Reading Football Club hold two notable records. In 1985/86 they won their first 13 games in Division Three. This is still the record for the most consecutive wins at the beginning of the League season in any division. They also hold the record for the longest run without conceding a goal. In 1978/79 they went for 1,074 minutes without conceding a goal, including 11 complete matches. Steve Death was the goalkeeper throughout the 11 games.

QUIZ QUESTIONS

Answers on page 48.

1. Who wrote:'I always pass on good advice. It is the only thing to do with it. It is never any use to oneself'? Regrettably, this attitude landed him in Reading Gaol.

2. How did Piper Island get its name?

3. Why were biscuit tins important to Reading?

4. What was the name of the Celtic tribe who lived in the Berkshire area at the time of the Roman conquest, and whose capital was just outside Reading?

5. Which king was buried in the church of Reading Abbey in 1136?

6. When did Reading become the county town of Berkshire, and which was the county town before that date?

7. What is the connection between the authoress Jane Austen and Reading?

8. An old story traditionally connects a Reading merchant with a measure of length. What is this story?

9. A Victorian replica of which famous piece of needlework can be viewed in Reading Museum?

10. Reading was once famous for its three Bs. What were they?

READING, QUEEN VICTORIA STREET 1910 62201

RECIPE

READING SAUCE

Mrs Beeton gave a recipe for Reading Sauce in her 'Book of Household Management':

('In using a jar of pickled walnuts, there is frequently left a large quantity of liquor; this should be converted into a sauce as below, and will be found a very useful relish.')

2½ pints (1500ml) of walnut pickle (or modern cooks might prefer to use mushroom ketchup, which is available from most supermarkets)

1½oz (45g) shallots

1 quart of spring water (946ml)

¾ pint (450ml) of Indian soy (soy sauce)

½oz (15g) of bruised ginger

½oz (15g) of long pepper

1oz (30g) of mustard-seed

1 anchovy

½oz (15g) of cayenne

¼oz (8g) of dried sweet bay leaves.

Bruise the shallots in a mortar, and put them in a stone jar with the walnut-liquor; place it before the fire, and let it boil until reduced to 2 pints. Then, into another jar, put all the ingredients except the bay-leaves, taking care that they are well bruised, so that the flavour may be thoroughly extracted;

put this also before the fire, and let it boil for 1 hour, or rather more. When the contents of both jars are sufficiently cooked, mix them together, stirring them well as you mix them, and submit them to a slow boiling for half an hour; cover closely, and let them stand 24 hours in a cool place; then open the jar and add the bay-leaves; let it stand a week longer closed down, when strain through a flannel bag, and it will be ready for use. The above quantities will make half a gallon.

Time - Altogether, 3 hours.

READING, CAVERSHAM LOCK 1912 64648

JOHN TIMS
& SONS
LANDING STAGE
FOR TOWN & STATIONS
BOATS HOUSED.

RECIPE

PORK BRAISED IN BEER

Berkshire is famous for the quality of its pork. To make this an even more local dish, use Courage's beer!

> 1.75-2.25kg/4-5lb loin of pork
>
> 15ml/1 tablespoon vegetable oil
>
> 25g/1oz butter
>
> 3 large onions, halved and thinly sliced
>
> 1 garlic clove, finely chopped
>
> 600ml/1 pint beer
>
> 1 bay leaf
>
> 1 tablespoon plain flour, blended with 2 tablespoons water
>
> Salt and black pepper

Season the pork on all sides with salt and pepper. Heat the butter and oil in a flameproof casserole just large enough to hold the pork. When hot, add the pork and brown on all sides for about 5 minutes, turning it to colour it evenly. Remove from the casserole and set aside. Drain all but 1 tablespoon of fat from the casserole. Add the onions and garlic and cook for about 5 minutes, until just softened. Stir in the beer, scraping to remove any bits on the bottom of the casserole. Add the bay leaf. Return the pork to the casserole, cover and cook over a low heat for about 2 hours, turning the pork halfway through the cooking time. Remove the pork from the casserole. Slice thickly, arrange on a platter and keep warm. Discard the bay leaf. Add the flour mixture to the cooking juices and cook over a high heat, stirring constantly, until thickened. Taste and adjust seasoning if necessary, pour over the pork and serve at once.

QUIZ ANSWERS

1. Oscar Wilde, who later wrote 'The Ballad of Reading Gaol'.

2. Piper Island is named after a local ferryman who lived there.

3. Reading was famous for the Huntley and Palmer biscuit works, which were once one of the town's biggest employers; their revolutionary idea was to put biscuits in tins, which solved the problem of keeping them fresh. For many years the Thames played an important role in the success of the firm, carrying biscuits downstream to London docks.

4. The Atrebates.

5. King Henry I was buried before the high altar of the abbey church in January 1136.

6. Reading took over from Wallingford as the county town of Berkshire in 1974.

7. Jane Austen and her sister Cassandra both went to the Abbey boarding school in Reading.

8. A tradition says that during the reign of Henry I (1100-1135) one of the richest of the great cloth merchants of England was Thomas of Reading. According to the story, the king met Thomas and his fellow merchants on the road one day, but their many wagons forced the king to move aside. At first he was angry; but then he realised how useful the support of such rich men might be. To win their favour, he established a standard measurement for cloth - the yard, which was exactly the length of his arm.

9. A replica of the Bayeux Tapestry.

10. Beer (Simonds' Brewery, later Courage's), bulbs (Sutton Seeds) and biscuits (Huntley & Palmer). All three businesses have now either closed or moved away.

CAVERSHAM, BRIDGE STREET 1908 59962

Did You Know?
READING
A MISCELLANY

Did You Know?
READING
A MISCELLANY

FRANCIS FRITH

PIONEER VICTORIAN PHOTOGRAPHER

Francis Frith, founder of the world-famous photographic archive, was a complex and multi-talented man. A devout Quaker and a highly successful Victorian businessman, he was philosophical by nature and pioneering in outlook. By 1855 he had already established a wholesale grocery business in Liverpool, and sold it for the astonishing sum of £200,000, which is the equivalent today of over £15,000,000. Now in his thirties, and captivated by the new science of photography, Frith set out on a series of pioneering journeys up the Nile and to the Near East.

INTRIGUE AND EXPLORATION

He was the first photographer to venture beyond the sixth cataract of the Nile. Africa was still the mysterious 'Dark Continent', and Stanley and Livingstone's historic meeting was a decade into the future. The conditions for picture taking confound belief. He laboured for hours in his wicker dark-room in the sweltering heat of the desert, while the volatile chemicals fizzed dangerously in their trays. Back in London he exhibited his photographs and was 'rapturously cheered' by members of the Royal Society. His reputation as a photographer was made overnight.

VENTURE OF A LIFE-TIME

By the 1870s the railways had threaded their way across the country, and Bank Holidays and half-day Saturdays had been made obligatory by Act of Parliament. All of a sudden the working man and his family were able to enjoy days out, take holidays, and see a little more of the world.

With typical business acumen, Francis Frith foresaw that these new tourists would enjoy having souvenirs to commemorate their days out. For the next thirty years he travelled the country by train and by pony and trap, producing fine photographs of seaside resorts and beauty spots that were keenly bought by millions of Victorians. These prints were painstakingly pasted into family albums and pored over during the dark nights of winter, rekindling precious memories of summer excursions. Frith's studio was soon supplying retail shops all over the country, and by 1890 F Frith & Co had become the greatest specialist photographic publishing company in the world, with over 2,000 sales outlets, and pioneered the picture postcard.

FRANCIS FRITH'S LEGACY

Francis Frith had died in 1898 at his villa in Cannes, his great project still growing. By 1970 the archive he created contained over a third of a million pictures showing 7,000 British towns and villages.

Frith's legacy to us today is of immense significance and value, for the magnificent archive of evocative photographs he created provides a unique record of change in the cities, towns and villages throughout Britain over a century and more. Frith and his fellow studio photographers revisited locations many times down the years to update their views, compiling for us an enthralling and colourful pageant of British life and character.

We are fortunate that Frith was dedicated to recording the minutiae of everyday life. For it is this sheer wealth of visual data, the painstaking chronicle of changes in dress, transport, street layouts, buildings, housing and landscape that captivates us so much today, offering us a powerful link with the past and with the lives of our ancestors.

Computers have now made it possible for Frith's many thousands of images to be accessed almost instantly. The archive offers every one of us an opportunity to examine the places where we and our families have lived and worked down the years. Its images, depicting our shared past, are now bringing pleasure and enlightenment to millions around the world a century and more after his death.

For further information visit: www.francisfrith.com

INTERIOR DECORATION

Frith's photographs can be seen framed and as giant wall murals in thousands of pubs, restaurants, hotels, banks, retail stores and other public buildings throughout Britain. These provide interesting and attractive décor, generating strong local interest and acting as a powerful reminder of gentler days in our increasingly busy and frenetic world.

FRITH PRODUCTS

All Frith photographs are available as prints and posters in a variety of different sizes and styles. In the UK we also offer a range of other gift and stationery products illustrated with Frith photographs, although many of these are not available for delivery outside the UK – see our web site for more information on the products available for delivery in your country.

THE INTERNET

Over 100,000 photographs of Britain can be viewed and purchased on the Frith web site. The web site also includes memories and reminiscences contributed by our customers, who have personal knowledge of localities and of the people and properties depicted in Frith photographs. If you wish to learn more about a specific town or village you may find these reminiscences fascinating to browse. Why not add your own comments if you think they would be of interest to others? See **www.francisfrith.com**

PLEASE HELP US BRING FRITH'S PHOTOGRAPHS TO LIFE

Our authors do their best to recount the history of the places they write about. They give insights into how particular towns and villages developed, they describe the architecture of streets and buildings, and they discuss the lives of famous people who lived there. But however knowledgeable our authors are, the story they tell is necessarily incomplete.

Frith's photographs are so much more than plain historical documents. They are living proofs of the flow of human life down the generations. They show real people at real moments in history; and each of those people is the son or daughter of someone, the brother or sister, aunt or uncle, grandfather or grandmother of someone else. All of them lived, worked and played in the streets depicted in Frith's photographs.

We would be grateful if you would give us your insights into the places shown in our photographs: the streets and buildings, the shops, businesses and industries. Post your memories of life in those streets on the Frith website: what it was like growing up there, who ran the local shop and what shopping was like years ago; if your workplace is shown tell us about your working day and what the building is used for now. Read other visitors' memories and reconnect with your shared local history and heritage. With your help more and more Frith photographs can be brought to life, and vital memories preserved for posterity, and for the benefit of historians in the future.

Wherever possible, we will try to include some of your comments in future editions of our books. Moreover, if you spot errors in dates, titles or other facts, please let us know, because our archive records are not always completely accurate—they rely on 140 years of human endeavour and hand-compiled records. You can email us using the contact form on the website.

Thank you!

For further information, trade, or author enquiries please contact us at the address below:

The Francis Frith Collection, Frith's Barn, Teffont, Salisbury, Wiltshire, England SP3 5QP.
Tel: +44 (0)1722 716 376 Fax: +44 (0)1722 716 881
e-mail: sales@francisfrith.co.uk **www.francisfrith.com**